# My Restaurant Scavenger Hunt

Bela Davis

T0026260

Abdo Kids Junior
is an Imprint of Abdo Kids
abdobooks.com

Abdo
Kids

SENSES SCAVENGER HUNT

**abdobooks.com**

Published by Abdo Kids, a division of ABDO, P.O. Box 398166, Minneapolis, Minnesota 55439.
Copyright © 2023 by Abdo Consulting Group, Inc. International copyrights reserved in all countries.
No part of this book may be reproduced in any form without written permission from the publisher.
Abdo Kids Junior™ is a trademark and logo of Abdo Kids.

Printed in the United States of America, North Mankato, Minnesota.

052022

092022

THIS BOOK CONTAINS
RECYCLED MATERIALS

Photo Credits: Shutterstock

Production Contributors: Teddy Borth, Jennie Forsberg, Grace Hansen

Design Contributors: Candice Keimig, Pakou Moua

Library of Congress Control Number: 2021950709

Publisher's Cataloging-in-Publication Data

Names: Davis, Bela, author.

Title: My restaurant scavenger hunt / by Bela Davis.

Description: Minneapolis, Minnesota : Abdo Kids, 2023 | Series: Senses scavenger hunt | Includes online
    resources and index.

Identifiers: ISBN 9781098261559 (lib. bdg.) | ISBN 9781644948361 (pbk.) | ISBN 9781098262396
    (ebook) | ISBN 9781098262815 (Read-to-Me ebook)

Subjects: LCSH: Senses and sensation--Juvenile literature. | Restaurants--Juvenile literature. | Scavenger
    hunting--Juvenile literature.

Classification: DDC 612.8--dc23

# Table of Contents

Restaurant
Scavenger Hunt . . . . . .4

Make Your Own
Scavenger Hunt . . . . .22

Glossary . . . . . . . . . . . .23

Index . . . . . . . . . . . . . .24

Abdo Kids Code . . . . .24

## Restaurant Scavenger Hunt

Let's go on a hunt! Can we find these things at a restaurant?

**1** metal thing

- - - - - - - - - - - - - - - - - - -

**2** baked taste

- - - - - - - - - - - - - - - - - - -

**3** clink sound

- - - - - - - - - - - - - - - - - - -

**4** green thing

- - - - - - - - - - - - - - - - - - -

**5** grilled smell

- - - - - - - - - - - - - - - - - - -

**6** cheesy taste

- - - - - - - - - - - - - - - - - - -

We have five **senses**. They can help find things.

7

I feel with my hand.

I feel a metal spoon.

I taste with my tongue.

I taste baked bread.

I hear with my ear.

I hear dishes.

I see with my eye. I see green **veggies**.

I smell with my nose.

I smell grilled burgers.

I taste with my tongue. I taste pasta with cheese. Yum!

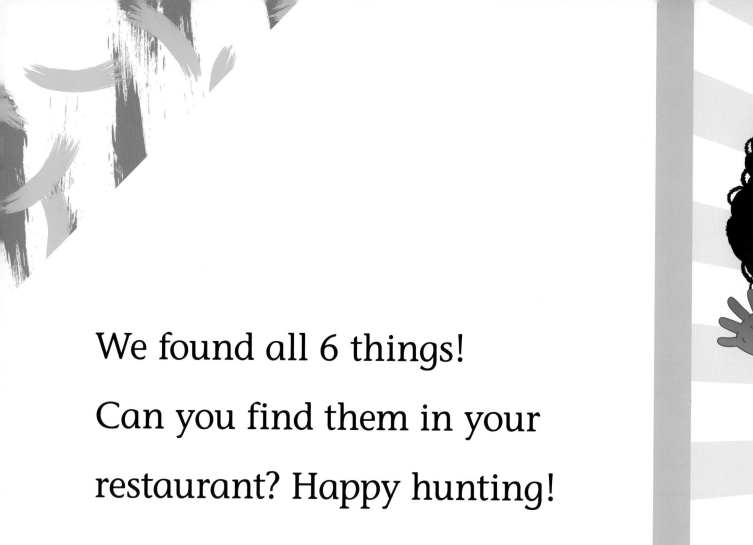

We found all 6 things!
Can you find them in your
restaurant? Happy hunting!

# Make Your Own Scavenger Hunt

**Decide Where to Go**

**Make a List of Things You May Find**

**Add Senses to That List**

**Find Your Things!**

# Glossary

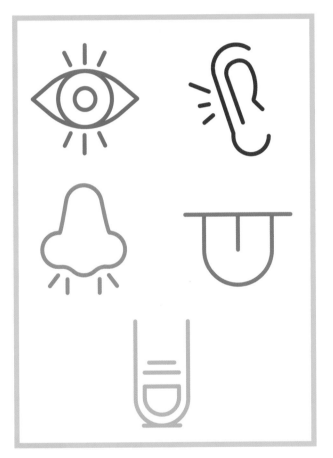

**sense**
any of five ways to experience one's surroundings. The senses are sight, hearing, smell, taste, and touch.

**veggies**
short for vegetables.

# Index

bread 10

burger 16

dishes 12

hearing 12

pasta 18

sight 14

smell 16

spoon 8

taste 10, 18

touch 8

vegetables 14

**Abdo Kids**
ONLINE
FREE! ONLINE MULTIMEDIA RESOURCES

Visit **abdokids.com** to access crafts, games, videos, and more!

Use Abdo Kids code

**SMK1559**

or scan this QR code!